— A FLAIR FOR HAIR —

A Flair for Hair

Tana Reiff

Grass Roots Press

A Flair for Hair
© Tana Reiff 2020
www.grassrootsbooks.net

Acknowledgements

Grass Roots Press acknowledges the financial support of the Government of Canada for our publishing activities.

Canadä

Produced with the assistance of the Government of Alberta through the Alberta Media Fund.

Albertan

Design: Lara Minja, Lime Design Inc.

Library and Archives Canada Cataloguing in Publication

Title: A flair for hair / Tana Reiff.
Names: Reiff, Tana, author.
Series: Reiff, Tana. Working for myself.
Description: Series statement: Working for myself | Originally published: Belmont, CA : Lake Education, ©1994.
Identifiers: Canadiana 20200241559 | ISBN 9781771533461 (softcover)
Subjects: LCSH: Readers for new literates.
Classification: LCC PE1126.N43 R444555 2020 | DDC 428.6/2—dc23

1

Beautiful for the Prom

"One more spray and you're done!" Jackie Jones said.

She was doing Taria's hair in her kitchen. The girl lived up the street. Taria was getting ready to go to the prom that night. Her mom watched every move as Jackie styled the girl's hair.

"She looks beautiful," said Taria's mom. "More beautiful than *I* ever looked for a prom!"

Jackie smiled. Taria *did* look beautiful. The girl was pretty to begin with. Now, with hundreds of curls around her face and down her back, she sparkled.

"Who are you going to prom with?" Jackie asked.

"Robert Tenby," said Taria.

"Well, I hope you have a wonderful time," Jackie said, smiling. "I hope you never forget this night."

Just then, Jackie's nine-year-old daughter Chloe came into the kitchen. "I'm going over to the store," said the little girl.

"OK," Jackie said. "You look both ways before you cross the street, you hear? And come right back home."

"I will, Mom," said Chloe as she skipped off.

"Do you remember your high school prom?" Taria's mom asked Jackie.

Prom was not something Jackie liked to talk about. Not her own prom, anyway.

"No, I don't remember," Jackie said. "Because I didn't go to the prom. I *wanted* to go. I even had a beautiful golden dress all ready to go. Then I made a big mistake. I got mad one day and just dropped out of school."

Tears came into Jackie's eyes. "The school wouldn't let me go to the prom after that," she said. "I still have that dress, though. It looks like new because I never did wear it."

"Here you are, doing hair for a prom," said Taria's mom. "And you never went yourself."

"The prom was a long time ago," said Jackie. "It doesn't matter anymore. What *does* matter is that I didn't finish high school."

"You seem to do all right for yourself and your daughter," said Taria's mom. "You get by with your job at Burger Bazaar. Seems to me you don't have it so bad."

"I don't want to flip burgers my whole life," said Jackie. "I wish I could be a real hairdresser. I'd like to make a living at it. That used to be my dream."

"Why isn't it *still* your dream?" Taria asked her. "You have a flair for hair!"

"Maybe so, but I would have to go to cosmetology school," said Jackie. "You know, beauty school. You have to learn all this stuff and then pass a test to get a license. I don't even have a high school diploma. I can't even think about all that now."

"There are ways," said Taria's mom. "You can still get your diploma. And then maybe you can dig up some money to go to cosmetology school."

"That all sounds too far for me to reach," said Jackie. "Maybe you're right. I really don't have it so bad the way things are. Could be a lot worse!"

"It's not too late to make your life better, you know," said Taria's mom.

Jackie handed Taria a mirror. "How do you like the back, honey?"

"I look like a princess!" Taria said, holding the mirror.

"Now, I want you and Robert to stop by here tonight, you hear?" Jackie said. "I want to take a picture of you in your prom dress with your princess hair."

Taria's mom started to hand Jackie some money. The same hairstyle would have cost twice as much in a salon. Still, Jackie wouldn't take the money.

"No, this is on me," Jackie said. "I do my neighbors' and family's hair for fun."

Later, Taria and Robert stopped by on their way to the prom. Jackie just about cried when she saw them. "Oh, you're *more* than a princess, honey. You two look like a king and queen!"

After Chloe left to stay over at a friend's house, Jackie ate dinner alone. Then she sat down to watch a movie. But her mind was somewhere else. *If only, if only, if only* kept going through her head. *If only* she had stayed in school. *If only* she hadn't been hanging out with Chloe's dad ten years ago. *If only* she hadn't had a baby when she was so young. *If only* she had taken cosmetology classes back in high school—and not dropped out.

Instead, Jackie was living paycheck to paycheck. Maybe her life wasn't so bad. But it wasn't so *great* either. She did not want to spend the rest of her life crying over what might have been.

There was a time when she dreamed about what she would do with her life. She tried to remember when she had stopped dreaming. Then she had a thought. Maybe dreaming was what she was starting to do again right now.

2

First Steps

Jackie was styling hair on a fake head. When she finished, her favorite teacher, Ms. Lucy, came over to take a look. "Good job, Jackie. Just even out the left side."

Jackie fixed the left side. Ms. Lucy signed Jackie's skill sheet.

Cosmetology school was like another world to Jackie. Ever since high school she had wondered what it would be like. Now she knew.

Not long after Taria's prom, Jackie started working on her high school equivalency diploma. For years, she had been pretty sure she would have to face the diploma matter sooner or later. If she wanted to become a licensed hairstylist, she would have to face it now.

So she started going to the adult education center to study for the diploma test. Classes were free and Jackie could choose her times to go there. She went to classes whenever she wasn't working at Burger Bazaar and Chloe was in school.

She was surprised at how much she remembered from high school. But math had always been hard for her, and it still was.

"I'll never make it to cosmetology school," she told herself over and over. She tried to stop herself from thinking like that. She needed that diploma.

And so she worked hard and started feeling smarter. She started telling herself, "I'm going to make it."

When the teachers thought she was ready, Jackie took a practice test online. She passed all but one part of the test. Of course, the one part she did not pass was math. That took more time to get ready for. But when she took the practice test again, she passed.

Then it was time to take the real high school equivalency test. Jackie spent most of the day taking all five parts of it. The next day, she checked her scores online. She had passed all five tests! Jackie had earned a high school diploma!

Proud as could be, she paid a visit to the school of cosmetology.

"I really want to study here," she told the supervisor. "I just don't know how I can pay for it."

"I'm sure we can help you get a job training grant," said the supervisor. "It will pay for everything."

The supervisor showed Jackie around the school.

One large room had hair styling stations along three walls. On the fourth wall was a row of shampoo sinks. Students worked on real people.

In another room were manicure tables. Rows of all colors of nail polish lined one wall.

There were classrooms where students watched a teacher show them how to do all kinds of things. At the front was a large screen for showing videos.

And in every room there were large pictures of beautiful hairstyles on the walls.

The supervisor talked as they walked around. "You'll be here eight hours a day," she explained. "Your only days off will be weekends and holidays. Do you think you can do that?"

Jackie knew this would be a big push. She would have to work evenings and weekends. She would have to ask her mother for more help with Chloe. But, after passing the high school test, she was on a roll. She had more drive now than ever in her whole life.

"Yes, I think I can do that," she told the woman. She said it slowly, but she was telling the truth.

"The new term starts soon," said the woman. "We'll work on getting that grant for you. You make your plans with work and childcare."

And then classes started. Full-time beauty school would take Jackie a whole year. She thought she might have to miss a day now and then. But she didn't. Beauty school was work and fun at the same time.

Jackie thought she already knew a lot about doing hair. But the very first day of school she found out there was much more to learn. This was cosmetology—not just hair, but nails and skin, too.

Right away, Jackie had to learn the rules of each area of cosmetology. There were laws to follow and all the students had to know them.

Next, she learned what hair, nails, and skin are made of and how they grow. The students had to know what they were working with and how to work safely.

Then came the fun part—styling. The class started with wet styling. Jackie learned how to feel people's hair. How to shampoo a head. How to pin curl and finger wave. How to braid and cornrow. How to weave hair. How to do hair extensions.

Jackie thought she knew how to comb hair. But she had to learn the *right* way to comb. And how to choose and use the right combs for different styles and types of hair.

And then she had to learn how to use oils and sprays and all kinds of hair products.

Next came classes on everything having to do with heat. How to blow dry. How to use a hood dryer. How to use a curling iron, a flat iron, hot rollers, and a hot comb.

After that came classes on how to give a perm. How to make spirals and spiky curls. And how to relax hair that was already curly.

A big part of the program was about how to cut hair. How to use scissors, a razor, clippers, and thinning shears. How to do short cuts, crops, layers, tapers, and feathering. How to shave lines and hair tattoos. How to do the popular cuts that everyone would ask for. How to clean and sharpen scissors. And how to do it all safely.

Jackie learned all of this, and enjoyed every minute.

Even more time went to hair color. At first Jackie thought, "Forty hours just on hair color?" But she was glad for that time. She learned how to do rinses, temporary color, and permanent color. How to do color streaks and how to strip color.

Jackie was also glad she had brushed up on math. She used it a lot when working with hair color.

A different teacher taught the last part of the course. In that class, Jackie learned how to give a facial. How to arch eyebrows. How to get rid of unwanted hair.

She loved the classes on makeup. Learning all about makeup made her feel like an artist.

Last of all, she learned how to do nails. Manicures for fingers. Pedicures for toes. She learned how to trim nails. How to file nails. How to color nails. How to do gel and shellac and dip powder. How to put on acrylic overlays and fake nails.

For ten years, becoming a licensed cosmetologist had seemed like a far-off dream. Now Jackie could almost reach out and touch that dream. Getting there was a matter of taking one step after another. One day at a time.

3

A License and a Job

Near the end of the cosmetology program, the students went out to visit real salons. Jackie visited two. One was very small. Only three people worked there, two women and one man. All of them were friendly to her. The place was busy but not noisy. Jackie liked the feel of it.

The second salon was downtown. It was called Hair Circus. Jackie counted 20 chairs, with 20 stylists working. The manager, Alonzo, said the place was always that busy. Jackie thought the name Hair Circus fit just right. That day, the big salon seemed *too* big for her.

But she went back to Hair Circus for a second visit. This time, Jackie styled someone's hair. Alonzo loved her work. "Lady, you style hair like an angel from heaven," he told her.

"I didn't know angels styled hair!" Jackie said, laughing.

She and Alonzo joked around like that all day. It made Jackie feel like part of the place. She began to like the feel of the big salon. Still, she never came right out and told Alonzo that she wanted to work there.

Back at the school, Jackie checked the job board. All the salons posted openings on it. Jackie would watch for one from Hair Circus. She wanted a job as soon as she got her license.

The end of the term came. Jackie had finished all her classes. But she couldn't work in the beauty field until she had a license. To get it, she had to pass the cosmetology board exam.

The test had two parts. For one part she had to write answers. For the other part she had to show what she could do.

There was a time when Jackie would have feared the written test. But after passing the high school equivalency test, she wasn't afraid. She was ready. And that first part of the test went well.

She didn't feel so sure about the second part. She had to show that she could do all the different things she had studied. The man giving the test watched her work on a fake head. He took notes as Jackie worked. By the end, Jackie knew she had done just fine.

It took time for the papers to come through. But then Jackie had her cosmetology license.

She got a frame and hung the license on her kitchen wall. There it was, with her name and picture right on it. She looked at it ten times a day. It would stay there until she found a job. Then she would take it to wherever she was working to hang on the wall there.

Jackie called her mom. "I shouldn't have a party till I find a job," Jackie said. "But I'm going to have one anyway!"

She asked all her neighbors and her family to come. She had done everyone's hair at one time or another. She wanted them all there to celebrate with her.

Jackie baked cakes and cookies all day. She made a fruit punch. She and Chloe cut pictures of great hairdos out of magazines. They hung them up all over the apartment.

People started showing up for the party. Many of them brought gifts.

"Will you still do my hair now that you have your license?" Taria asked.

"Sure, honey," Jackie said. "But you'll have to bring yourself downtown to a salon when I get a job!"

Jackie played music real loud. Everyone danced and had a good time. Jackie hadn't had that much fun for a long time.

The next week, Jackie went back to the beauty school to check the job board. She went back again and again. She waited to see a posting from Hair Circus. Still nothing.

"Does Hair Circus always tell you when they have a job opening?" she asked.

"Oh yes, they do," said the school supervisor. "But why don't you just go and visit them again?"

Jackie took the bus downtown to Hair Circus. The place was as busy as always. "I really want to work here," she told Alonzo.

"We don't have an opening right now," he said. "Tell you what. Give me your number and I'll let you know if something opens up."

"Really?" Jackie couldn't believe Alonzo would do that. *He must like me,* she thought.

"I just hired a new stylist a few weeks ago," said Alonzo. "She had a following from another salon. So she brings in clients to Hair Circus. But I like your work better than hers. I would have picked you if I knew you wanted to work here."

"Why wasn't there a posting on the job board?" Jackie asked.

"Because she happened to walk in the day someone else quit," Alonzo explained. "She was in the right place at the right time, I guess."

"Well, call me, OK?" said Jackie.

"Lady, I have your number," said Alonzo. He gave her a thumbs up and waved as she left the salon.

Sure enough, only a week later, Alonzo called. He asked Jackie to come work at Hair Circus. The money wasn't great, but there would be tips. Jackie gave Burger Bazaar two weeks' notice. Her boss was sorry to see her go. She had always been one of his best workers.

The first week on the new job, Jackie had fun, even though her feet felt heavy from standing so much. But the day she cashed her first paycheck from Hair Circus, those same two feet felt as light as air.

If she hadn't just had a party, she would have one now. Instead, she just kept saying to herself, "Is this really happening to me?"

4

Circus at the Circus

Jackie had not met many new people since leaving high school. When she wasn't at work, she had spent most of her time with Chloe. Jackie took her to the park just about every day back then. As the kids played, she talked with the other young mothers from the neighborhood.

On weekends, she saw her mom and neighbors and cousins. She hadn't made any real friends at Burger Bazaar. Most of the workers were younger than Jackie—just kids, really.

So working at Hair Circus was a new world for Jackie. She liked the idea of everyone working together. But, because it was new to her, she didn't always do and say the right things.

Ivan worked the chair next to hers. From the first day, Jackie didn't like him. Even so, she should have kept her mouth shut.

"He's such a little jerk." That's what Jackie said about Ivan to the client she was working on. The woman didn't say anything.

Jackie finished styling her hair. The woman went up front to pay. Alonzo took her credit card. "How was everything?" he asked.

The woman answered, "My hair is fine. But Jackie is saying things about one of your other stylists."

Alonzo was not happy to hear that. "Thank you for telling me," he said. "I hope you'll come back again soon."

"If I do, I'll ask for someone else to do my hair," the client said.

After she left the salon, Alonzo came over to Jackie. "Lady, we can't be bad-mouthing each other," he told her. "Would you want another stylist talking about *you*?" He wasn't joking this time.

Jackie wished she could sink into the floor. "I was out of line," she said. "It won't happen again."

It didn't happen again. But Jackie did get into trouble with Lila, the stylist at the station on the other side of her.

Lila was off sick the day Carl Morgan came in for a haircut. Lila had cut Carl's hair for two years. He never called ahead for an appointment. He just dropped in and asked for Lila. But Lila wasn't there that day, and he wanted his hair cut anyway.

"Hey, lady," Alonzo said, "Can you fit in another cut right now?"

"Sure," Jackie said.

Carl Morgan sat down in Jackie's chair. She felt his hair. "A little dry," she said to him. "You might want an oil treatment today."

"Fine," Carl said. "Go ahead."

Jackie cut his hair and gave him an oil treatment. Carl went crazy over the great job she did.

"I never looked so good!" he said. "I'm going to ask for you from now on." He gave Jackie a big tip on top of his bill.

The next time Carl came in, he asked for Jackie. Of course, Lila saw Carl sitting in Jackie's chair. After he left, Lila said, "What do you think you're doing, stealing my client? He's a good tipper!"

"I didn't steal him," Jackie said. "You weren't here the last time, and he asked for me this time."

But Lila was still angry. She asked Alonzo to move her to a different styling station. Whenever Carl came in, Lila would give Jackie a dirty look.

So there were bad days. But Jackie loved having a full-time job with day hours. She loved spending time with Chloe after work.

As the months went on, Jackie noticed that Carl came in more often than he needed to. She began to think he was coming in to see *her*—not just to get a haircut.

At last, one day Carl said, "Hey, Jackie. You and me, we know each other pretty well by now. Would you like to go out with me sometime?"

Jackie hadn't been on a real date since one time when Chloe was little. She had sort of given up on men. But Carl Morgan seemed nice. Jackie *did* like him. And he was very good looking, especially after she did his hair. Hair Circus had no rules about dating clients. So she said, "OK."

After that, Jackie's life *really* changed. She started seeing Carl every week, then every night. Chloe really liked him, and he liked Chloe. Carl's two sons loved Jackie. They needed a mother in their life.

When they decided to get married, no one was surprised. Up until then, Jackie had not thought much about getting married—to anyone. But Carl was a nice guy with a good job. They really loved each other and had so much fun together. The idea of marrying him felt right.

Not only did Jackie and Carl get married, but they also bought a house. It had three bedrooms, a small yard, and even a basement. It was in Jackie's old neighborhood.

All of a sudden, Chloe had two brothers. And Jackie had a new husband, a new home, and three kids. Now she had people around her every night of the week.

She also had a job that seemed to give her a new problem every day.

5

New Plans

Alonzo was the manager of Hair Circus, but not the owner. One day he called a meeting of the stylists. The owner wanted Alonzo to tell everyone about a new plan.

"You'll be getting paid in a new way starting next week," Alonzo explained. "You won't get paid by the hour anymore. From now on, you'll be paid by the head. You'll get a share of all the money you bring in for Hair Circus, based on how many clients you have."

After a year on the job, Jackie wasn't sure she liked the sound of this new plan. "Suppose that Lila and I are both here for eight hours. Are you saying that we might get paid different amounts?"

"That's right," said Alonzo. He didn't sound happy about it. But it was his job to carry out the owner's wishes, like it or not.

"Think of it this way," he added. "Suppose you have a really busy day. Then you would make *more* than you did before."

"But what if the weather is bad and no one shows up?" Lila asked. "Then we sit here for nothing. That's not fair."

"The owner thinks this *is* the fair way," said Alonzo. "And as you build your 'book,' you'll have the same clients coming back over and over. The more clients who ask for you, the more money you'll make. Plus, you'll get a cut on any products that you sell."

So that was that. The stylists had to live with the new plan or leave Hair Circus.

Ivan left before the new plan even started. Lila didn't leave, but she moaned about it every day. "Would you like cheese and crackers with your whine?" Alonzo asked her. That made Jackie laugh. But she kept it to herself. She had learned her lesson a long time ago.

Jackie didn't know how the new plan would work out for her. Her book was pretty full and she got a lot of walk-ins. Her old friends came in often, and every week she picked up new clients.

As it turned out, Jackie made out well on the new plan. At first.

Then one day, while she was cutting a man's hair, she felt sick. She said, "Excuse me, sir. I'll be right back." She went in the back room and sat down. She took a deep breath. She came back to her styling station. Even though she didn't feel good, she finished cutting the man's hair.

That sick feeling came and went over the next few days. Jackie knew what was going on.

It had been more than 12 years since she was pregnant with Chloe. She had almost forgotten what it felt like. This *did* feel different. *A different baby*, she thought. *A different father.* And she was 12 years older.

Jackie and Carl were very happy about having a baby. But Jackie was really sick with this one. Many mornings she just couldn't make it to work on time.

Sometimes she had to turn over clients to other stylists. Having fewer clients, when you're paid by the head, was costing her money. The products didn't smell as good as they used to, either.

And the talk! Jackie and Carl didn't want anyone to know about the baby. Not yet. But the buzz started anyway. Lila must have started it. Every time Jackie walked by her station, Lila would stop talking. Jackie was sure the talk was about her being pregnant.

One night at home, Carl said to Jackie, "I've been thinking. We have that whole basement down there. Maybe we could finish it off. We could make it into a family room."

"I've been thinking about the basement, too," Jackie said. "I wonder if we could turn it into a little salon. That way, I could work at home, with the baby and all."

Carl really wanted a family room, but he saw Jackie's point. "Do you think you can make as much money working at home?"

Jackie thought she could charge less but make more. There would be no one taking part of the money. "I already have a lot of my own stuff," she said. "Scissors, combs, blow dryer, rods. I'd have to put out some money to get started. I'd need a shampoo sink and a styling station and a chair and a big mirror. And I'll have to buy insurance, in case anyone gets hurt by mistake."

"It will also cost some money to fix up the basement, you know," said Carl.

"Right. But we both know you have to spend money to make money. So what do you think?" Jackie asked her husband.

"It's OK with me," said Carl. "But we'd better get started before you get too big."

"Uh, yeah," said Jackie, patting her baby bump. "We're going to have to start by getting a business license."

Leaving Hair Circus might not be as quick and easy as it sounded.

6

Everything in Order

Jackie knew how to style hair. But she didn't know how to set up a salon. She found a checklist online. It explained all the steps she would need to follow.

First, she applied for a zoning permit.

The basement would need its own door to the outside. Clients would not be allowed to come in through the house. Luckily, Jackie and Carl's house had a basement door.

There would have to be a bathroom in the basement. They didn't have that. So they had a small bathroom put in. A water line ran to the shampoo sink. And they put in a fan to pull air from inside to outside.

The zoning permit came through. But it did not allow Jackie to put up a sign outside. No problem. She didn't have a sign and would not get one.

Next, she had to decide what kind of business her salon was going to be. She decided to be a "sole proprietorship." In other words, she was the one owner and proprietor—the person running the business.

She also had to get a sales tax number. She would have to collect sales tax on her services and any products she sold, and then pay those taxes.

And Jackie would have to set up a "doing business as" name, or DBA. She filled out a form online. She would be called simply "Jackie Jones Morgan, DBA Jackie's Salon."

"All of this paperwork is a lot of trouble," Jackie said to Carl.

"Are you sure you want to go through with it?" Carl asked.

"I've come this far," said Jackie. "I might as well go all the way."

"OK," said Carl. "Just thought I'd better ask."

And so she and Carl turned the basement into a hair salon.

They found a good buy on flooring. They bought paint. Jackie found out about a salon that was going out of business. She bought their shampoo sink, a styling station with built-in mirror, a chair, and towels—all for next to nothing.

The sink needed a new hose, so she bought one at a beauty supply store. While she was there, she bought clips, hairpins, masks, gloves, and two shampoo capes.

When the basement was all set up as a salon, she called the cosmetology board. They sent out a person to inspect Jackie's Salon. It passed the inspection with flying colors. They gave Jackie a certificate.

Jackie was still working at Hair Circus while all this was going on. And, as everyone could now see, she was pregnant—and getting bigger every day. It was not an easy time, but she felt really good about her plan to go out on her own.

Now, everything was in order to apply for an in-home business license. Jackie answered all the questions on the application. She included her new zoning permit, along with the cosmetology board certificate and her cosmetology license.

The last thing she did was buy insurance. Everything was set to go. She had done everything right.

When the license came, she put it in a frame and hung it on the wall next to her cosmetology license.

Then it was time to break the news to Alonzo. He was surprised and sorry to see her go. He tried to make a joke of it.

"You *are* good," he told her. "But running your own business is no day at the park. You'll come crawling back. Just you wait and see."

Jackie laughed. "I'm much too pregnant to crawl," she said.

Still, she knew she would miss some things about Hair Circus. She would miss learning from the other stylists. She would miss walk-in clients who came back because they liked her work. She would miss seeing how a business runs. Most of all, she would miss Alonzo.

7

Home But Not Alone

"Hi, Jackie! It's me, Taria!"

"Hi, honey. It's been a while. Come on in and have a seat," said Jackie. "How about this? Here I am doing your hair in my own home again."

"Different home, though," said Taria, looking around.

"*Real* different!" Jackie laughed. "I have a great husband, four kids, and two licenses now." She pointed to the cosmetology and business licenses on the wall. It made her feel proud just to look at them. She showed them to everyone who came in.

"What do you want me to do with your hair today?" Jackie asked Taria.

"I want my curls relaxed a little," Taria said. "And I want you to do my hair so my ears won't stick out."

"I hear you," said Jackie. She started combing Taria's hair. She always tried to listen to what clients wanted. Then she would add her own ideas for getting the style just right.

"What's your baby's name?" Taria asked. She peeked at the sleeping baby.

"Rochelle," said Jackie. "I named her after my Aunt Rochelle."

"Pretty name," said Taria. "Pretty baby, too."

"I'm going to use cocoa butter to relax your curls," said Jackie. "I don't use strong chemicals with the baby around. The cocoa butter will make your hair really soft and loosen up the curls."

"That's sounds good to me," said Taria.

Jackie put cocoa butter all through Taria's hair. Then she wrapped it in a hot towel.

"OK, now we wait 30 minutes," said Jackie. "So we have time to talk. Let's hear about you and Robert. Are you planning to tie the knot any time soon?"

"He hasn't asked me yet," said Taria. "He wants to finish trade school before we get married. He's going into construction."

"And what about you? What kind of work would *you* like to do?" Jackie asked.

"I used to think about going on to some sort of school," said Taria. "But I haven't thought much about that since Robert and I got together."

"Well, don't forget about your own dreams," said Jackie. "Sometimes you have to reach out and grab what you want."

When Taria's hair was finished, it was soft, with nice, loose curls. It looked longer than before the cocoa butter. "Perfect!" Taria said, looking in the mirror.

"Check or cash today, honey?" Jackie asked.

A look of surprise came over Taria's face. "Oh," she said softly. "I didn't bring a check *or* cash. Now that you're working at home, I thought..."

"That's OK," Jackie said. "You don't have to pay me."

"Thanks! You're like the big sister I never had!" said Taria. She gave Jackie a big hug. "See you soon!"

After Taria left, Jackie got to thinking, and made up her mind. "It's fine to help people out once in a while," she said to herself. "But if I don't charge the people I know, I'll go out of business in no time at all."

The next morning, Jackie found money from Taria stuck in the door. There was a note with it. "Sorry I acted like a deadbeat. Hope we're still friends. Love, Taria." Jackie smiled. Her mom must have talked to her.

That Sunday, a crowd of Jackie's family came over to see the baby. As it was just about time to leave, Aunt Rochelle said, "OK, everyone. Let's line up. Before we go, Jackie can cut everyone's hair."

Jackie thought Aunt Rochelle was kidding—but she wasn't. "You can all hate me," Jackie began, "but I can't cut everyone's hair. For one thing, this is my day off. And for another thing, I've made up my mind. The only heads I do for free are the people who live in this house."

Aunt Rochelle put her hand over her mouth in surprise. She couldn't believe that Jackie would say such a thing. But Jackie was glad she had spoken up for herself.

She didn't see Aunt Rochelle for a long time after that. But all the others came to her salon, one by one. Every one of them paid for Jackie's services. Jackie did, however, give them a family discount.

And when Aunt Rochelle heard there was a discount, she came to get her hair done like all the others had. But really, she couldn't stay mad at Jackie. And she couldn't have found a better hair stylist if she tried.

8

A Business Plan

At first, most of Jackie's Hair Circus clients had come to her home salon. Some of them still did. Others stopped coming.

Jackie wasn't getting walk-in clients, as she had at Hair Circus. She didn't have Alonzo giving her new clients. So it was getting hard to fill up her appointment book. She needed to build up her business with new clients.

It was also time to renew the cosmetology license. To do that, she would have to take a course. She wanted to learn more about how to run a salon. So she signed up for the manager course. The cosmetology school had day care for Rochelle.

It was good to be back in class.

"Is that you?" said Ms. Lucy, Jackie's favorite teacher. "You look so different!"

"Oh, it's me," Jackie said. "Been through some changes since I saw you last. I worked at Hair Circus. Got married. Bought a house. Had another baby. And now I'm running my own salon in my basement."

"Wow!" said Ms. Lucy. "Those *are* a lot of changes. So you're here for the manager course?"

"I am," said Jackie. "I have my salon up and running, but I need to build up my business. I need more clients. I thought maybe I could learn about all that here."

"You sure will," said Ms. Lucy. "You'll learn how to market your business. And a whole lot more. Like how to set up times for clients to come in. How to buy the things you need for the salon. How to manage other stylists. How to do the books. All that stuff. You'll even learn how to write a business plan."

So, as part of the manager course, Jackie wrote a business plan for her salon. She decided how much money she would try to make in the next two years. She decided what she would need to do to reach that point. She decided how much she would have to spend to get there. Learning to run and market the business was all part of the plan.

Jackie soaked up everything she learned in the class. Every time she got a new idea at school, she tried it out at home.

The first thing she did was to put a sign on the wall. It listed her services with a price for each one.

Then she started selling shampoo and other hair products. She set up a display. Anyone walking in or out couldn't miss seeing it. Of course, Rochelle knocked it over every other day. When that happened, Jackie just set the display back up again.

Soon after the manager course was over, Jackie tried some new marketing ideas.

One was a special deal for clients. Anyone who sent her three new people got a free haircut. She did two free cuts the first month. That brought in six new clients.

Then one day a woman stopped in, not to get her hair done but to sell advertising. The advertising would be space on a large mailing piece full of ads for different businesses and services. The ad could be small, so it wouldn't cost too much. The woman said it would be mailed to every home for miles around. And that the ad would surely bring Jackie new business.

Jackie decided to buy the smallest size ad. It said "Jackie's Salon—Hair with a Flair," with her picture and phone number. It also said "20% off your first visit." Jackie thought that said it all. People could cut out the ad and bring it in to get the discount.

"Look at that!" she said as she showed her ad to Carl.

Now there was nothing to do but wait for new clients to call. And they did. The mailer was good advertising without spending a lot of money.

And then there was the matter of braids. As they told her in class, it was good to have one thing you were known for.

"Hey, Jackie," a client asked one day. "Do you know how to do that new kind of braid? I don't know what it's called."

"There are a lot of cool braids," Jackie said.

"I saw a picture and I want it for myself," said the client. She pulled out her phone and showed Jackie a photo.

"It so happens that I'm going to a class on braiding next week," said Jackie. "I'll see if I can learn how to do that one."

Sure enough, Jackie learned how to do 34 kinds of braids. And she was good at every one of them. Word got around. She got so busy, she didn't know what to do.

9

More Than Enough

Dance music played as Jackie wrapped thick cornrows around Taria's head.

"Every time I do your hair it's a little more fancy than the last time!" Jackie said. "So where are you going this time? Tell me all about it."

"My cousin's wedding," said Taria. "Robert is coming with me, of course."

"Not making your own wedding plans yet?" Jackie asked.

"Maybe next year," said Taria. "He's still in school. And I want us to be really sure about each other before we get married."

"Honey, that is nothing but smart," Jackie said.

"Thanks, Jackie," said Taria. "I mean, plenty of my friends are with the wrong guys. Some of them have babies and they're not doing too great. And you—well, you're doing fine now. But it wasn't easy, was it?"

"Nothing is ever easy," said Jackie. "But it's a whole lot harder when you have to raise a kid by yourself."

"Not everybody ends up as lucky as you," said Taria.

"Yeah," Jackie agreed, laughing. "You can say I'm lucky. But remember—I worked for everything I have."

Taria started moving to the music.

"Hold still, honey," said Jackie. "I can't get this row straight if you're dancing!"

"The music makes me feel like I'm in a downtown salon," said Taria.

"I only have the dance music on for *you*," said Jackie. "Most of the time I play real soft music. If clients want a downtown salon, they have their pick. You want a nice, quiet space, where no one but me sees them getting their hair done? Then Jackie's Salon is the place to be."

Jackie finished Taria's hair. She handed her a mirror. "I love it!" said Taria with a hug. "You're the best, Jackie!" Taria paid and left.

When the next woman came in, Jackie changed the music. After that, a man came in. The last appointment of the day was another woman, right after the man left.

That's how all of Jackie's days were now—full. Every time a new mailer went out, she got calls. She stopped the free cuts deal because she didn't need the extra business. She had more clients than time to work on them. She was booking clients weeks ahead and working Saturdays.

Then one Saturday she was combing out a client she first met at Hair Circus. "I miss going downtown to get my hair done," the woman said. "I wish you still worked at Hair Circus."

That put an idea in Jackie's head. Some of her clients would *rather* go downtown. They might run into friends or go out to lunch after getting their hair done.

As she was thinking, a loud noise started upstairs.

"What in heaven's name is going on up there?" the client asked.

"It's just Carl," said Jackie. "It's the weekend. He and the kids are home."

"Sounds like he's roller skating up there!" said the client.

"Our wood floors are kind of loud," said Jackie.

"Well, just so long as he doesn't come down here," said the client. "I wouldn't want your husband to see me with a head full of rollers!"

The client couldn't hear what Jackie was thinking. *It's his house, too,* went through her mind. What Jackie said out loud was, "It's just one of those things you put up with when your business is at home."

Then they heard Chloe and the boys running back and forth upstairs.

Just then, Carl came down to the basement to get Rochelle. The client hid her face. "If you tell anyone you saw me looking like this, I'll never speak to you again!" she told Carl.

"Why don't I take a picture and post it for the world to see?" Carl laughed. He started to reach for his phone.

"No! No! Stop!" said the woman.

"I'm just joking with you," Carl said. He was trying to be a good sport. But really, he often wished that people weren't coming in and out of the house all the time. He could do without the laughing and music coming from the salon. He picked up Rochelle and went back upstairs.

"Hey, Carl," Jackie said that night. "I've been thinking. Maybe I should rent a shop downtown. It would get the salon out of the house. Some people would rather go downtown anyway. And I could hire other stylists. Maybe Jackie's Salon has outgrown this house."

"Say you went out and rented a shop," Carl said. "Say you had all the space you needed. Say you hired one or two people. Are you ready for all that? Are you ready to be a salon manager?"

"I took the manager course."

"I know. But what I'm asking is this—do you really want to run a downtown salon?" Carl asked. "That would be a whole new ball game."

"Yeah," said Jackie. "It would. Maybe I'm being crazy."

10

Sweet Dreams

The next morning, just for kicks, Jackie looked at rental listings. In the Shops for Rent section, she saw three that looked interesting. After work, she went to see them. Just for kicks.

The first two were out of the question. Too big. Too rundown. Too close to bad businesses. Too far away from restaurants. Something was very wrong with both of them.

The third shop got Jackie's wheels turning. As soon as she walked in, she could see herself working in that space. She could picture at least two other styling stations set up along the walls. She could see a waiting area for clients.

She could see walls covered with gold paper that wasn't even there. She could see a shiny black and white checkered floor where there was just a plain green one now. Everything about the place seemed right to her. Even the price.

"I'll think about it," she told the man who showed her around.

"Better think fast," said the man. "Shops on this block don't stay empty for long!"

She waited until the man left and walked away. Then she stepped into the shop next to the one for rent.

"I'm Jackie Morgan," she began. "I was wondering if you knew anything about the space for rent next door."

"That shop has been empty for months," said the shopkeeper.

"Oh, really?" Jackie said. "Do you know the landlord?"

"He's all right," said the woman. "He owns this building too, so he's also my landlord. He's just trying to get a higher price than that shop is worth. Maybe you can talk him into a lower rent, like I did."

"Thanks," said Jackie. "I'm glad I talked to you."

For the next few days, Jackie could think of nothing but that downtown shop. *A downtown salon would be the greatest thing in the world,* she told herself. Then she would think, *Who do I think I am, thinking I can run a successful downtown salon?* Then the other Jackie would kick in and say, *What is holding you back from your dreams?*

She talked to Carl about it.

"Why don't you wait a week before you do anything?" Carl said. "Give yourself some time to think. If this shop doesn't work out, something else will come along."

"Good thinking," Jackie said.

So Jackie waited a week before calling the landlord. *Maybe he'll come down on the price,* said one side of her. *If the rent is too high, then this was not meant to be*, said the other side.

She asked the landlord if he would take a lower rent. Much lower. He said no, but he would take $50 less than he was asking. Jackie asked if he would take $150 less. He said no, but he would take $100 less and that was as low as he would go.

Jackie said, "Fine. It's a deal. When can I move in?"

She hung up the phone and sat there in shock. "Well, you did it now, girl," she said to herself.

Just then, Taria burst in the door. "I have big news! I thought I had *one* big thing to tell you, but I have *two*!"

"Let me guess," said Jackie.

"Yes!" Taria said. "Robert asked me to marry him! Next month he finishes trade school at last! And he got a job with a construction company!"

"That's wonderful!" said Jackie as she gave Taria a big hug. "When?"

"June 24th," said Taria. "Save the date!"

Taria went on and on about her wedding plans. Then she said, "You'll do my hair for the wedding, won't you?"

"Of course I will, honey," said Jackie. "It will be my wedding gift to you!"

Taria hugged Jackie hard. Then she started to leave.

"Wait!" Jackie called after her. "What's your other news?"

"Oh, I almost forgot! Remember when you told me to reach out and grab what I want? No, I didn't ask Robert Tenby to marry me. But I *did* make up my mind about something else. I've decided to go to cosmetology school. I want to follow in your footsteps!"

Jackie grabbed Taria by both hands. "That's just great, honey! Now let me tell you *my* news. I'm moving my salon downtown. And you know what? Just as soon as you get your cosmetology license, there will be a job waiting for you in my new place!"

Jackie and Taria were like two little girls, jumping up and down. They hugged each other five or six more times.

At last, Taria said, "I have to go. Put me down for the whole morning of my wedding day. I just know you are going to give me the best braids ever!"

"I can't wait," said Jackie.

The next four months were busy like never before. Jackie got a bank loan to buy new styling stations, shampoo sinks, supply trolleys, and so many other things.

Carl helped Jackie put in a new floor and hang gold wallpaper. Every night they worked on the new downtown salon. All the kids helped, except little Rochelle. She just played on a soft floor mat. Jackie had a sign painted: *Jackie's*, it said, in fancy gold letters.

Jackie hired two stylists who had just finished beauty school.

She set up a Facebook business page. Her first posting announced the "Grand Opening of Jackie's."

She bought food and drink and plates and cups. She hung rows of gold ribbon across the shop. This was going to be a good party.

And she asked Taria to do *her* hair this time.

Everything about the grand opening party was perfect.

"This place looks like prom night," Taria said. "And look at you, Jackie. You're the prom queen!"

Jackie was wearing her golden dress. It was the one she had kept all these years, from the prom she never went to. "Thanks, Taria," she said. "Can you believe I can still fit into it?"

"Let tonight be your prom night!" Carl told his beautiful wife. "May I have this dance, lovely lady?" He took her hands and danced around the salon with her.

Jackie couldn't remember ever feeling this happy. All that had happened came rushing through her head. Dropping out of school. Having Chloe when she was still so young. Working at Burger Bazaar.

And then getting her high school diploma. Studying for her cosmetology license. Working at Hair Circus. Finding Carl. Starting her own salon at home. Having Rochelle. Building her business.

And now this—a beautiful downtown salon of her own.

Yet Jackie knew that these things had not just "happened" to her. She had made everything happen, through her own hard work. Just a little later than some people.

"I must be dreaming," she said out loud. Her eyes were a little wet as she spoke.

"Are you all right?" Carl asked her.

"Oh, yes," said Jackie. "I'm more than all right. Nothing could be better than all this. I just want to keep dreaming, that's all. I can't ever let the dreaming slip away."

Carl took Jackie's hand and held it tight. "That's why I love you," he said to her softly. "You make dreams come true."

Jackie would see ups and downs in her business. There would be good days and bad days ahead. But tonight ... tonight was a night to celebrate how far she had come and how far she could go.

Made in the USA
Middletown, DE
21 May 2021

40159833R00031